PORSCHE

FAST AND BEAUTIFUL

by
SHIRLEY HAINES
and
HARRY HAINES

THE ROURKE CORPORATION, INC.
Vero Beach, FL 32964

ACKNOWLEDGMENTS

The authors and publisher wish to express their appreciation to the Porsche Automobile Company for invaluable assistance in compiling the pictures and technical information for this book. Special thanks are due to Paul Schinhofen and Thomas Nagaba (Porsche, A.G., Stuttgart) and Martha McKinley (Porsche Cars North America, Inc.) for their extra time and effort in locating missing photographs.

A big thank you is due the following Porsche owners who allowed their cars to be photographed and included in this book: Amarillo Precision Porsche for the 928 found on the cover, pages 4 and 23; Ron Snelgrove for the 356B on page 13; A.G. Papp for the 911T on pages 14/15 and the Carrera on page 31; and to Billie Hunt for the 924S on pages 20/21.

Thanks to Ken Parker for the drawing on page 11.

PHOTO CREDITS:

Porsche: Ferry Porsche/356/911 on page 5, Porsche #1 on page 6, the 3 "Ferdinand Porsches" on page 7, aerial view of the factory on page 8, 356A, drawing and emblem on pages 10/11, 356B on page 12, 911s on pages 16/17, 914 and drawing on pages 18/19, 928 on page 22, 944s on pages 24/25, racing cars on pages 26/27, and all pictures on pages 28/29.

Harry Haines: 928 on the cover and page 4, production line photos on page 9, 356B on page 13, 911T on pages 14/15, 924 on pages 20/21, 928s on page 23, and the Carreras on page 31.

Library of Congress Cataloging-in-Publication Data

Haines, Shirley, 1935-
    Porsche: fast and beautiful / by Shirley and Harry Haines.
      p. cm. – (Car classics)
    Includes index.
    Summary: Gives a brief history of the Porsche automobile and describes its special features and classic models.
    ISBN 0-86593-143-7
    1. Porsche automobile – Juvenile literature. [1. Porsche automobile.] I. Haines, Harry, 1932- . II. Title. III. Series: Car classics (Vero Beach, Fla.)
TL215.P75H33 1991
629.222'2 – dc20
                                      91-7643
                                         CIP
                                         AC

CONTENTS

CHAPTER 1

PORSCHE: HOW DO YOU SAY IT?

Porsche. How do you say it? "PORSCH-eh."

While the name may be hard to pronounce, the cars need no introduction. Even people who know little or nothing about automobiles will recognize a Porsche because Porsche cars have always been different.

Almost all car manufacturers build a variety of two-door and four-door models. Porsche, however, has never made anything but a two-door sports car. When practically all sports cars were powered by

A 1987 Porsche 928S. Still in production today, it is the largest Porsche and one of the most copied automobiles of the 1980s.

Pictured above is Dr. Ferry Porsche, who headed the company for many years, with the two cars that have the longest production runs. On the left is the model 356, which was produced from 1948 to 1965. At the right is a recent model 911 which began production in 1965 and is still the company's most popular car.

water-cooled engines in the front, Porsche used air-cooled engines in the rear. While other automobiles changed models each year and tried to make them look different, Porsche built their original car for almost 18 years.

Porsches are definitely special. This company's unique approach over the years has created an air of mystery, and even reverence, toward its automobiles. The Porsche design has become famous.

CHAPTER 2

FERDINAND PORSCHE: A FAMILY AND ITS CARS

The first Porsche. Completed in June, 1948, it was a two-seater built mostly with Volkswagen parts. Powered by a 4-cylinder, air-cooled engine of 1131 cc, it was rated 35 hp at 4000 rpm. Top speed was reported as 85 mph.

Porsches are made by a family-owned company, led by a father, son and grandson, all named Ferdinand Porsche. The father, Ferdinand Anton Porsche, was born in 1875 in Czechoslovakia, then called Bohemia. When he was only 25, he designed and built his first car. Called the Lohner-Porsche, it was electric-powered and won a number of races. For the next thirty years, Porsche worked as an auto designer for a number of companies. He is best remembered for the Mercedes S models, which were among the finest cars of the 1920s.

In 1931 Dr. Porsche established his own company in Stuttgart (SH-toot-gart), Germany. It was an independent consulting business that specialized in the design of automobiles. One of the employees was

Ferdinand Anton Porsche, 1875-1951, one of the most famous names in the history of the automobile worked for Mercedes in the 1920s. He designed the well-known S and SS models and was principal designer of the Volkswagen Beetle. Surprisingly, he had comparatively little to do with the cars that bear his name.

Ferdinand Anton Ernst "Ferry" Porsche was born in 1909. Principal designer of the model 356 and head of the company until 1972, he served as head of the Board of Advisers, 1972-1990. More than any other person, Ferry Porsche has been the leader of the family and the company. He is now Honorary Chairman of the Board.

Ferdinand Alexander "Butzi" Porsche was named Chairman of the Supervisory Board of Porsche AG on March 9, 1990. Eldest son of Ferry, he worked for the company from 1957 until the family resignation in 1971. During the period from 1961 to 1971, he was head of Porsche design and responsible for the company's best-known car, the Porsche 911.

his son, Ferdinand "Ferry" Porsche. In May, 1934, the German government hired the Porsche company to design a "people's car," which they named Volkswagen. Three prototypes were built in the garage of the Porsche home and shown all over Germany in the late 1930s. By the time the factory was ready, however, Europe was at war and no cars were being built. Very few cars had been built before the war started.

Following the war, Dr. Porsche was held prisoner by the French until August, 1947. By then, he was a tired, ill, old man. During this period, his son, Ferry Porsche, designed a little two-seater sports car. He called it the "Porsche 356" because it was the 356th design since the company had originated in 1931. The car was completed in June, 1948 and a few weeks later won a local race in Innsbruck, Austria – the first ever Porsche racing victory. Dr. Ferdinand Anton Porsche suffered a stroke in November, 1950 and died on January 30, 1951.

Ferry Porsche, his sister and their families continued to manage the company until the early 1970s. Then, because they feared that family favoritism might hurt the business, management was turned over to trusted employees in 1972. The Porsches became stockholders only.

CHAPTER 3

PORSCHE AG: THE COMPANY

Pictured above is an aerial view of the Porsche factory. Visitors who would like a tour must write ahead for an appointment. A small museum is located on the factory grounds. Many of the photographs in this book are of cars on display in the museum.

The Porsche company likes to think of itself as the largest of the small automobile firms that manufacture sports cars to a worldwide market. The current product line features three basic cars. They are the 928, Porsche's big car, the 911 or Carrera, with air-cooled rear engine, and the 944 series, powered by a 4-cylinder water-cooled front engine. Approximately 30,000 new Porsches are built each year. The production reported at the 1990 Supervisory Board meeting, for instance, was as follows:

Car	Number	Percentage
Porsche 911	17,019	55%
Porsche 944	10,450	34%
Porsche 928	3,426	11%
TOTAL	30,895	100%

Work on the production line. One look tells you these are all Porsche 911s. This is the most famous profile in sports car history.

Porsche cars are sold all over the world, but the United States continues to be the largest market. The company employs approximately 8,400 people. Of these, about 2,200 (26%) work at the Porsche research and development facility in Weissach (VEES-saw-sh), Germany, a village outside of Stuttgart. No other automobile firm has such a large percentage of employees working on research. Porsche's heavy commitment to research probably stems from two factors. First, the original company, started in the 1930s, did research for other automobile companies, and research is a company tradition. Second, Porsche has a major involvement in racing and needs a large facility for testing its competition cars. There is no question that the company's outstanding cars are directly related to its major commitment in research.

Stuttgart, Germany is one of the most famous automobile manufacturing centers in the world. Mercedes-Benz and a number of other companies have major plants located in this city of approximately 600,000 people. All Porsche road cars are made in Stuttgart. Racing cars are made at the Research Center in nearby Weissach.

HAMBURG

BERLIN

GERMANY

FRANKFURT

STUTTGART

MUNICH

CHAPTER 4

THE CAR THAT BUILT PORSCHE: MODEL 356

The very first Porsche featured an engine mounted in front of the rear axle. Only one car like this was ever built, and even while it was under construction, Ferry Porsche was planning a car that would be more practical.

The new design placed the engine behind the rear axle, as was currently being done with the Volkswagen. This placement simplified the manufacturing process and also allowed considerably more luggage space. A coupe and cabriolet (convertible) were planned. No one knew it at the time, but this design would last for the next 18 years.

Production of the 356 reached only 4 cars in 1948, 25 cars in 1949, and 18 cars in 1950. The main reason for the slow production was body construction since each car was built by hand in Gmünd, a small village in Austria. The Porsche family moved the company back to Stuttgart, where materials and workers were available for a true production line. The first German-made Porsche was completed on Good Friday in 1950.

Production increased so rapidly in Stuttgart that on March 15, 1954, the 5,000th Porsche was driven off the line. During the 1950s, changes and improvements were constant. A larger engine was offered at 44 hp, and hydraulic brakes, a one-piece windshield and a fully synchronized transmission became standard on all models. Stronger bumpers were set out from the body and, at the suggestion of the American distributor, Max Hoffman, the Porsche emblem was established.

So many improvements were taking place that the company decided to create a new model designation. In October of 1955, the first 356A was built. The car shown at right is a 1956 Porsche 356A that has been completely restored and is displayed today in the Porsche Museum in Stuttgart.

The Porsche emblem, which is so well known today, was established in 1952. Its background is the crest of the State of Baden-Wurttemburg, the part of Germany where the plant is located. In the center is the coat of arms of Stuttgart – a rampant black horse on a yellow shield. The horse represents the old area of Stuttgart, which had been a stud farm (Stuotgarten, from which the city takes its name).

A 1956 Porsche 356A 1600 S Coupe. The most noticeable new features were the curved windshield and 15-inch wheels. At that time, 70 percent of all Porsches were exported, a figure that allowed the company to expand rapidly in the post war economy.

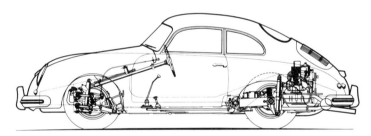

Cutaway drawing of the first version of the Porsche 356A Coupe

Technical Data

Engine	4-cylinder, air-cooled, opposed-piston engine, central camshaft with push rods, 8.5:1 compression
Output	75 hp at 5000 rpm
Displacement	1582 cc
Fuel system	Mechanical fuel pump, 2 Solex downdraft carburetors
Driveline	Fully synchronized, 4-speed Porsche gearbox
Chassis	Unitary, all-steel body, independent suspension, torsion bars, hydraulic drum brakes
Dimensions	Wheelbase 2100 mm, length 3950 mm
Weight	850 kg
Performance	Top speed 175 km/h (109.4 mph)

CHAPTER 5

ENDING AN ERA: MODEL 356

The early 1960s were the golden years of the 356 series. The range of body styles was the widest ever and included coupes, cabriolets, two-seater roadsters and a hardtop-coupe with a fixed roof. The company produced 7,598 cars in 1960, 7,664 in 1961, 8,205 in 1962, and a total of 9,672 in 1963.

The car pictured here is a 1963 Model 356B 1600 Coupe. While other Porsches of the day had larger engines (the Carrera, a racing version, had a souped-up 135 hp edition), the regular sedan still came with the 60 hp standard model. Other technical details are given in the box on the facing page.

An important step in Porsche history came in 1961 with the construction of the company's new

A 1963 Porsche 356B 1600 Coupe. This particular car is on display at the Porsche Museum in Stuttgart. The yellow-colored glass in the headlights was probably not standard.

Another 1963 model 365B. These photographs give a good representation of the last two versions of a car that was made for almost 18 years. The 356C, introduced in late 1963, offered only a few details that were different.

proving ground at Weissach. This was to grow eventually into a massive complex that could put all cars through their paces, from secret prototypes for large manufacturers to Porsche's own designs. Today, 26 percent of all Porsche employees work at this facility for research and development.

The year 1963 marked the beginning of the end for the model 356. From that time on, the new 911 began to dominate. The last model 356 came off the assembly line in 1965. For a design that was expected to sell only 500 cars, the 356 had become a miracle. When the last car rolled away, it was number 76,303. From 1948 to 1965, the model 356 literally built the company.

Technical Data

Engine	4-cylinder, air-cooled, opposed-piston engine, central camshaft with push rods, 7.5:1 compression
Output	60 hp at 4500 rpm
Displacement	1582 cc
Fuel system	Mechanical fuel pump, 2 Solex downdraft carburetors
Driveline	Fully synchronized, 4-speed Porsche gearbox
Chassis	Unitary, all-steel body, independent suspension, torsion bars, hydraulic drum brakes
Dimensions	Wheelbase 2100 mm, length 4010 mm
Weight	950 kg
Performance	Top speed 160 km/h (100 mph)

CHAPTER 6

RISKING THE COMPANY: MODEL 911

In the early 1960s, Ferry Porsche made the most important decision in the history of the company. He assigned his son, Ferdinand "Butzi" Porsche, to develop the drawings of the successor to the model 356. This was a tremendous gamble. Stopping production of the car that had built the company and replacing it with a new, unknown design meant risking the future of the company.

A model 911, the most famous of all Porsches and possibly the most recognized sports car profile in automotive history. The model 912 looked the same but was equipped with a smaller engine.

This beautifully maintained 1972 model 911T was 18 years old when these photographs were taken. It is a classic example of the high regard Porsche owners have for their cars and the basis for their superb resale value, which has been maintained over the years.

When the new car was shown for the first time at the Frankfurt Auto Show in September, 1963, it created a sensation. It had just enough family likeness to the 356 to be recognized as a Porsche, yet the fresh new design and the many improved features won immediate public acceptance. Among the improvements were greater interior space, 50 percent more glass area, and, most importantly, a larger and more powerful 6-cylinder engine.

The design was originally called the model 901. However, Peugeot, the French automobile company, filed an official complaint saying that they had rights to the number. While the car remained the same, Porsche simply changed the number to 911.

The first cars reached the market in September, 1964. Only one model was available, a two-door sedan. In later years two other models were added.

When the 911 was introduced for sale in the fall of 1964 as a 1965 model, it was priced at $5,496. This was about $1,500 more than the old model 356 had cost, and some people felt that the high price was eliminating many potential buyers. A quick solution was to install the old 1600 cc, 4-cylinder engine (the one used in the model 356) in the new body and lower the price. This variation was called the 912 and was introduced to the U.S. market in September 1965 as a 1966 model.

Technical Data	
Engine	6-cylinder, air-cooled, opposed-piston engine, 2 chain-driven overhead camshafts
Output	130 hp at 6100 rpm
Displacement	1991 cc
Fuel system	6 Solex overflow carburetors
Driveline	5-speed Porsche gearbox
Chassis	Unitary, all-steel body, independent front suspension, disk brakes, rack and pinion steering
Dimensions	Wheelbase 2111 mm, length 2163 mm
Weight	1080 kg
Performance	Top speed 210 km/h (131.25 mph)

CHAPTER 7

PORSCHE'S GREATEST SUCCESS: 911

A new chapter in the history of the Porsche company began in September, 1964 when the first 911 rolled off the line. Now, in the 1990s, time has proven this car to be Porsche's most popular model and one of the most outstanding sports cars ever built. The 911 has the most famous profile of any sports car and is the auto most people recognize as a Porsche.

Changes have been continuous over the years, and the present 911 has few if any technical similarities to the original. The engine, in particular, has undergone many improvements, almost always to increase power and speed. A comparison of the box on the facing page with the technical data on the previous page will show that the current 911 and the original 911 really are two different cars.

Over a quarter of a century after the 901 was first shown to the public, the basic body shell remains unchanged. Under the skin, everything is different, but the total look today is not unlike that of 1963.

Above left: A 911 Targa as it looks in the 1990s. Porsche invented the concept of a detachable top and named it for a race in Sicily. The word, and the auto style, are now used worldwide by all auto manufacturers.

Above right: Finally, a true convertible (Porsche calls it a cabriolet) for the 911 series appeared in 1982. Except for the top itself, all three 911 models are the same mechanically and in most other respects.

The designation "targa" is used to describe a car that has a removable center top but retains the passenger protection of a car body for the area just behind the driver. Usually, the back part of the car roof contains a roll-bar or some kind of structure to protect passengers in case of an accident. "Targa" was a word developed by Porsche and first used in 1966 on their model 911 cars. The name was taken from an annual race held in Sicily called the Targa Florio. A true convertible or cabriolet was not introduced for the 911 series until 1982.

The 1990 version of Porsche's air-cooled, 6-cylinder engine that has made history with the model 911 and all of its variations.

Technical Data

Engine	6-cylinder, air-cooled, horizontally-opposed, single overhead camshaft per cylinder bank, 11.3:1 compression
Output	250 (DIN) hp at 6100 rpm
Displacement	3600 cc
Fuel system	Bosch L-Jetronic with Digital Motor Electronics
Driveline	Fully synchronized, 5-speed Porsche gearbox
Dimensions	Wheelbase 2272 mm, length 4250 mm
Weight	1350 kg
Acceleration	0 – 100 km/h (0 – 62.5 mph), 5.7 seconds
Performance	Top speed 260 km/h (161 mph)

CHAPTER 8

THE MID-ENGINE CARS: MODEL 914 AND OTHERS

In the late 1960s, Porsche was enjoying great success with mid-engine racing cars. Mid-engine placement offers numerous advantages for a racing car. The three major advantages are:

(1) Compactness, with resulting light weight that aids acceleration and reduces braking effort.

(2) Low polar moment of inertia from a central grouping of the major heavy components (which makes the responsiveness better).

(3) Good weight distribution.

Porsche, Volkswagen, and Karmann, three of the most respected auto companies in Germany, all believed there would be a new market for a mid-engine sports car. In the late 1960s the three companies entered into an agreement to produce the model 914 jointly. This new car would use Porsche engineering, Volkswagen engine, and Karmann bodywork. Public introduction of the 914 was made at the Frankfurt Auto Show in September, 1969, and the first cars reached American showrooms in March, 1970.

Artist's drawing of the layout of the 914/8. There were two trunks for luggage, a large one in front and a small one at the back, behind the engine.

Technical Data

Engine	8-cylinder, air-cooled, opposed-piston engine, 4 chain-driven overhead camshafts 7.5:1 compression
Output	300 hp at 8200 rpm
Displacement	2997 cc
Fuel system	Mechanical fuel injection
Driveline	Fully synchronized, 5-speed Porsche gearbox
Chassis	Unitary, all-steel body, independent suspension, torsion bars
Dimensions	Wheelbase 2450 mm, length 3985 mm
Weight	1050 kg
Performance	Top speed 250 km/h (156.25 mph)

The 914, Porsche's mid-engine car. The car pictured here was the personal car of Ferry Porsche.

The original 914 came with the new VW "traditional" 4-cylinder (opposed), air-cooled overhead-valve engine. The more powerful 914/6 shared the 6-cylinder, single overhead cam engine with the 1968-69 911T. Later an 8-cylinder version, called the 914/8, was produced. The car pictured here is a 914/8 that was given to Dr. Ferry Porsche on the occasion of his sixtieth birthday. He drove it as his personal car for more than 10,000 kilometers; it now resides in the Porsche Museum in Stuttgart.

For a number of reasons the 914 series did not sell well, and production lasted only six years.

CHAPTER 9

RADICALLY NEW: MODEL 924

A 1988 model 924S. When introduced in 1975, this was the first road car offered by Porsche with a water-cooled engine in front.

When the model 924 was introduced in 1975 it was the most radical departure in the 28-year history of Porsche. The company that had established its reputation by building cars with air-cooled engines in the rear was now unveiling its newest car with an engine neither air-cooled nor in the rear. Could a car with a water-cooled engine in front be a Porsche? Some people thought not!

The Porsche design staff, led by Harm Lagaay, was responsible for the body design. It featured an amazingly low Cd (coefficient of drag) of 0.36, one of the best in the world at that time.

People who have trouble telling this car from the 944 have good reason. The body work is almost identical.

Offered at first with only a 4-speed manual shift, within the year this was upgraded to a 5-speed manual. Then Porsche introduced another startling item – a 3-speed automatic transmission.

The 924 was produced initially with a VW engine. It was a small 4-cylinder engine with 1984 cc rated at 95 hp. In order to fit the low hood design, the motor was slanted to the right at a 40-degree angle.

The big news for 1979 was the introduction of a turbo version. This boosted the engine to 143 hp at 5500 rpm. Both the 924 and the 924 turbo remained basically unchanged through 1981 when production ended for U.S. models.

In June, 1986, the 924 reappeared as the 924S. The body was the same as before, but the engine, drive train, brakes, suspension and electrical system were all taken from a later model, the 944. The 924S claimed a top speed of 134 miles per hour and, with the 5-speed manual transmission, 0 – 60 mph in 8.3 seconds. But even the new 924S was a bit of a disappointment. Porsche didn't like the sales figures, and customers didn't like the performance. In 1988, after only 2 years, the 924 was permanently discontinued.

Technical Data for 1988 Model 924S

Engine	4-cylinder, water-cooled engine, single overhead camshafts, 10.2:1 compression
Output	158 hp at 5900 rpm
Displacement	2479 cc
Driveline	Fully synchronized, 5-speed Porsche gearbox
Dimensions	Length 4290 mm, width 1785 mm, height 1275 mm
Weight	1240 kg, 2734 pounds
Performance	Top speed 215 km/h (134 mph) Acceleration 0 – 100 km/h (0 – 62.5 mph) 8.4 sec

CHAPTER 10

PORSCHE'S BIG CAR: MODEL 928

The 928 is Porsche's largest, most powerful, and most expensive car. In the thirty-year period since World War II, the 928 was the first-ever car to be designed from a clean sheet of paper as an all-Porsche Porsche. No borrowed parts from VW, no imitation of any previous body shape – it was all-new, period.

First shown to the public at the Geneva Auto Show in March, 1977, the 928 was different from any other car on the road or anything else at the show. The 928 was a dazzling new car that received an enthusiastic reception from the people and the press.

Driver convenience was outstanding and considered state of the art for 1977. An adjustable steering wheel (up and down) took the instrument cluster with it when raised or lowered. Also, it had power windows, a central locking system, air conditioning, cruise control, 4-speaker stereo, rear-window wiper with 2-stage electric defogger, retractable headlights and headlight washers,

Pictured here are the two models currently offered: The Porsche S4 (with automatic transmission) and the Porsche 928GT (with 5-speed stick shift). Except for the transmission and the wheel design, the cars are identical. As expected, performance is slightly better from the 928GT.

electrically adjusted and heated outside rear view mirrors and sun visors for the rear seat passengers. A central warning system monitored fluid levels, lights and break pad wear. If a customer wanted a button, light, or gauge, the 928 had it. All of this gadgetry was installed in a car of superb technical engineering and design. The box below gives technical information for the 1990 model 928GT.

Since 1977, Porsche has consistently been improving its new water-cooled engine and chassis design. The company's goal, no doubt, is to reach a similar state of perfection that it achieved with the air-cooled, rear-engine cars.

A 1987 model 928. The changes made from year to year are present, but only an expert can find them. This continuity of model design is good for resale value, and Porsche cars are among the highest in the industry.

Technical Data for 1990 Model 928GT

Engine	Ninety degree V-8, water-cooled engine, 4 overhead camshafts, 4 valves per cylinder, 10.0:1 compression
Output	330 hp at 6200 rpm
Displacement	4957 cc
Fuel system	Bosch LH-Jetronic electronic fuel injection
Driveline	Fully synchronized, 5-speed Porsche gearbox, rear wheel drive
Dimensions	Wheelbase 2500 mm, length 4520 mm
Weight	1580 kg
Performance	Top speed 275 km/h (170 mph) Acceleration 0 – 100 km/h (0 – 62.5 mph) 5.8 sec

CHAPTER 11

PORSCHE FOUR-CYLINDER: MODEL 944

A 1990 model 944 S2 Cabrio.

The introduction of the 944 in September, 1981 is remembered for the enthusiastic reception given by automotive writers. *Autoweek, Car and Driver, Motor Trend, Road and Track*, and *VW and Porsche* all wrote about the new car as if employed by Porsche's advertising agency. These superlatives were well founded; the 944 was everything the 924 should have been. Eight months later Porsche introduced the U.S. version in May, 1982 as a 1983 model.

A key to the success of the 944 has been its 4-cylinder, water-cooled engine. The initial performance numbers were 2479 cc, 150 hp at 5500 rpm for American delivery. Now, almost 10 years later, the 2479 remains the same, but the other numbers have increased. The turbo version is rated at 250 hp at 5800 rpm. Complete technical data is given in the box on the facing page.

The 1990 944 S2 Coupe and 944 Turbo.

People who have difficulty recognizing the 944, especially being able to separate it from the 924, have good reason. The basic body shell and chassis for the 944 were taken directly from the 924 and 924 turbo. The interiors are also much the same. Other than the heater control, the early 944 dash looked almost identical to that of the 924.

Some writers contend that the 944 will be the Porsche that brings the old-guard, air-cooled, engine-in-the-rear Porsche fans into the world of water-cooled drivers. To date, this has not happened as the 911 continues to outsell the 944 by a big margin (and at a larger price). But the 944's performance is better in almost every way.

The 944 S2 Engine. One of Porsche's most successful engineering achievements is this little 4-cylinder, water-cooled power plant.

Technical Data for 1990 Model 944 Turbo

Engine	4-cylinder, water-cooled engine, single overhead camshafts, 8.0:1 compression
Output	250 hp at 5800 rpm
Displacement	2479 cc
Fuel system	Bosch L-Jetronic DME electronic fuel injection
Driveline	Fully synchronized, 5-speed Porsche gearbox, rear wheel drive
Dimensions	Wheelbase 2400 mm, length 4230 mm
Weight	1400 kg
Performance	Top speed 260 km/h (161 mph) Acceleration 0 – 100 km/h (0 – 62.5 mph) 5.9 sec

CHAPTER 12

RACING CARS

The Porsche name and competition are synonymous. The very first Porsche was barely a week old when it was entered in a race and won. Since then hardly a day, a week, or a month has gone by without Porsches winning something, somewhere.

Pictured on these two pages are three racing cars that were big winners in the 1970s and 1980s. They were "company cars," as opposed to privately owned, and are now on display in the Porsche Museum in Stuttgart.

Porsche said they were only entering the 1973 World Championship for Makes to "gain information about the further development of the model 911." The 911 Carrera RSR entered the famous 24-hour Daytona, Florida endurance event and won easily, beating more powerful prototypes from Ferrari, Matra, and Mirage-Ford.

The Porsche 935 won the World Championship for Makes in 1976 and 1977. After 1977, the company decided to retire from world endurance racing and instead sell cars to customers who wished to enter these races. Many did buy Porsche race cars, and privately owned 935s won the World Championship for the next four years. The exception to Porsche's "retirement" from the racing world was the Porsche 935/78. It was a variation of the 911, with an aerodynamic body so large it was called "Moby Dick."

The 956, pictured here, is regarded as a fourth-generation Porsche racer and a milestone in design. Three models of this car were entered at Le Mans in 1982 and won unrepeatable first, second, and third places. A number of technological developments have been derived from this car for use with the company's road autos.

Porsche 911 Carrera RSR. The hottest car on the racing circuit, it won everything there was to win in 1973.

Technical Data for
1973 Porsche 911 Carrera RSR

Engine	6-cylinder, air-cooled, 2-valve, normally-aspirated engine, 2 chain-driven overhead camshafts
Output	330 hp at 8000 rpm
Displacement	2992 cc
Fuel system	Bosch mechanical injection pump
Driveline	Fully synchronized, 5-speed Porsche gearbox, rear wheel drive
Dimensions	Wheelbase 2271 mm, length 4235 mm
Weight	900 kg
Performance	Top speed 280 km/h (175 mph) Acceleration 0 – 100 km/h (0 – 62.5 mph) 4.0 sec

Porsche 935/78 Coupe. In 1978 this car used the most powerful version of the Porsche "six" and came with water-cooled heads for the first time in company history.

Technical Data for
1978 Porsche 935/78 Coupe "Moby Dick"

Engine	6-cylinder, air/water-cooled, 4-valve, opposed, turbo engine, 4 cogwheel-driven overhead camshafts
Output	750 hp at 8200 rpm
Displacement	3211 cc
Fuel system	Bosch mechanical injection pump
Driveline	4-speed gearbox, no differential
Dimensions	Wheelbase 2279 mm, length 4890 mm
Weight	1025 kg
Performance	Top speed 365 km/h (228 mph)

Porsche 956C Coupe. In the years 1982, 1983, 1984, and 1985, the model 956 was regarded by the press as the most successful racing car in the world.

Technical Data for
1982 Porsche 956C Coupe

Engine	6-cylinder, air/water-cooled, 4-valve, opposed, turbo engine, 4 cogwheel-driven overhead camshafts
Output	620 hp at 8200 rpm
Displacement	2649 cc
Fuel system	Fully electronic, performance-optimized, Bosch fuel injection
Driveline	5-speed gearbox
Dimensions	Wheelbase 2650 mm, length 4800 mm
Weight	820 kg
Performance	Top speed above 350 km/h (above 218 mph)

CHAPTER 13

THE YEARS AHEAD

Porsche could easily build its future by continuing to produce more of the same. The company's three major lines are distinct and offer a wide selection of choices:

- ❏ Porsche 928, V-8, the big car, $75,000 – $80,000
- ❏ Porsche 911, 6-cylinder air-cooled engine in the rear, $50,000 – $60,000
- ❏ Porsche 944, 4-cylinder water-cooled front engine, $40,000 – $50,000

Left: This photo was supplied by Porsche in response to the question, "What are the company's plans for the future?" The official response: "Porsche is working on a number of ideas."

All three models appear to be selling well. One might expect the company to drop the 911 because of its 1963 design and air-cooled engine. As one critic noted, recently, "Nobody else builds an air-cooled engine anymore!" But the 911 is the sales leader, and all public bets are that it will still be around well into the next century.

Racing continues to be a major interest for Porsche. With Porsche's "Indianapolis 500 involvement" getting bigger each year, competition cars and engines are likely to become even more important to the company. Also, Porsche's super car, the 959, may be offered on more than a limited basis in the future.

The 1991 product line. For the 1990s, Porsche will continue to produce three distinct model lines. They are the 4-cylinder (water-cooled engine in the front) 944, the 6-cylinder (air-cooled engine in the rear) 911 Carrera 2 and Carrera 4, and the V-8 (water-cooled engine in the front) 944.

Porsche AG, however, was built on a tradition of research, innovative ideas and risk. When a company commits 26 percent of its work force to research and development, new ideas are bound to emerge. Given the past history of the company, one or two of these new ideas may even revolutionize the automobile business.

CHAPTER 14

PORSCHE: IMPORTANT DATES

1875 Ferdinand Anton Porsche is born September 3 in Maffersdorf, Bohemia.

1900 Lohner-Porsche electric car introduced at the Paris World's Fair. Hub motors built into the front wheels make Porsche's name known around the world.

1909 Ferdinand (Ferry) Porsche is born September 19 in Wiener-Neustadt, Germany as second child of Ferdinand and Johanna Porsche.

1923 Ferdinand Porsche is named technical director at Daimler (later Mercedes-Benz) in Stuttgart. Over the next five years many outstanding Porsche designs are created, including the now-famous SSK and SSKL Mercedes sports cars.

1924 Dr. Ferdinand Porsche receives an honorary doctorate from the Stuttgart Technical Institute.

1931 Ferdinand Porsche founds an independent company to design automobiles. Its offices are in Stuttgart, and one of the employees is Ferry Porsche.

1935 The German government commissions the Porsche company to build a "people's car." In German, this term is written as "Volkswagen." Three prototypes are running by the end of the year.

1936 Ferdinand Porsche receives an official contract to plan and design a new factory for building Volkswagens.

1938 Cornerstone is laid on May 26 for the Volkswagen factory at Wolfsburg, Germany.

1939 The first Volkswagen is presented at the Berlin Automobile Show. War begins and production is halted.

1940-1945 World War II dominates Germany. Ferdinand Porsche works on various military projects including the Leopard, Tiger and Maus tanks. Stuttgart is heavily bombed. Ferry Porsche and the Porsche family move the Porsche offices to an old sawmill in Gmünd, Austria.

1947 First major postwar contracts: (1) a Grand Prix race car, (2) a water turbine, and (3) a sports car for an Italian company called Cisitalia.

1948 The first car to bear the Porsche emblem is completed and named the "Model 356" because it is the 356th design of the Porsche company since its beginning in 1931.

1949 After building 50 cars, the Porsche family relocates the company to Stuttgart.

1950 The first German-built Porsches begin to roll off the production line in Stuttgart. Dr. Porsche celebrates his 75th birthday only to suffer a stroke two months later.

1951 Dr. Ferdinand Anton Porsche dies, January 30. Porsche starts for the first time at the 24-hour race in Le Mans and wins its class.

1954 The 5,000th Porsche leaves the factory on March 15. The company begins talking about a new design to replace the Model 356.

1963 A new Porsche designed by Ferdinand Alexander (Butzi) Porsche, then called Model 901 but later named 911, is introduced at the Frankfurt Automobile Show.

1965 The last Model 356 rolls off the production line. It is #76,303, the car that built the company. Ferry Porsche is awarded an honorary doctorate by Vienna Technical University.

1966 On September 21, the 100,000th Porsche rolls off the line. It is a Model 912 outfitted for police work.

1969 The mid-engine 914 is introduced as a combination VW/Porsche with body by Karmann.

1972 Porsche AG is turned into a stock company as the family withdraws from active management. Weissach Research and Development Center opens.

1973 Porsche competes in turbocharged racing cars by introducing the 917/30. With a 12-cylinder turbo engine rated at 1100 hp, it is the most powerful car ever built for the racing circuit.

1974 Porsche presents the 911 Turbo, the first production sports car in the world with turbocharging. It produces 260 hp from a 3-liter engine.

1976 Porsche develops an alternative to its classic air-cooled, rear-engine construction style. The Model 924 is introduced with a water-cooled front engine.

1978 The 928, introduced the previous year, becomes the first sports car chosen "Auto of the Year."

1981 Model 944 is introduced in the firm's 50th anniversary year.

1983 At the Frankfurt Auto Show, Porsche introduces the Group B competition car (later the Model 959) featuring all-wheel drive and many new technology improvements.

1986 Three Porsche 959s entered in the Rallye Paris-Dakar win places 1, 2, and 6.

1988 The 911 Carrera 4 with electronically controlled 4-wheel drive is introduced to mark the 25th anniversary year of the 911.

1990 On March 9, Ferdinand (Butzi) Porsche is named Chairman of the Supervisory Board of Porsche AG. His father, Ferdinand (Ferry) Porsche, becomes Honorary Chairman.

GLOSSARY

cabriolet (CAB-ree-o-lay) – A car with a canvas top that can be folded down, a convertible.

cc – Cubic centimeters. The amount of space in the engine cylinders. The larger the number of cc's, the larger the engine and power.

dohc – Dual overhead cam. Two drives (instead of one) that operate the levers or cams that open and close the valves and are located over the head of the engine.

km/h – Kilometers per hour. The speed of a car in kilometers.

mph – Miles per hour. The speed of a car in miles.

Stuttgart (SH-toot-gart) – The city in Germany where Porsche automobiles are made.

syncromesh (SIN-crow-mesh) – A gearbox design that helps to align the gears of an auto and makes shifting easier and smoother, from the word synchronize.

Weissach (VEES-saw-sh) – A small village near Stuttgart where the Porsche Research and Development Plant is located.

INDEX